IT'S TIME TO FOCUS ON THE WORD OF GOD

RONALD DAUGHERTY

IT'S TIME TO FOCUS ON THE WORD OF GOD

THE KEY
TO TRANSFORMED THINKING

RONALD DAUGHERTY

Lithonia, GA

© 2019 Ronald Daugherty
All rights reserved.

No part of this publication may be reproduced, stored in a retrieval system or transmitted in any form or by any means, electronic, mechanical, photocopying, recording or otherwise, without the expressed written permission of the publisher.

Scripture references are taken from the King James Version of the Holy Bible unless otherwise noted.
Pronouns for referring to the Father, Son and Holy Spirit are capitalized intentionally and the words satan and devil are never capitalized.

Publisher:
More Excellent Way Enterprises
www.mewellc.com

The Key to Transformed Thinking
Second Edition
ISBN: 978-1-7334383-6-0

Library of Congress Control Number: 2020903728

Printed in the United States of America

*To all those who are pursuing peace and
tranquility in difficult times…*

TABLE OF CONTENTS

Foreword ix

Introduction xiii

Chapter 1 1

Transformation – a transition in form, nature, or character – going from one behavior to a better one through process and time

Chapter 2 15

Holiness – making the right choices consistently

Chapter 3 23

Meditation – thinking about the solution until the answer is rooted in your subconscious

Chapter 4 31

Baptism in the Holy Spirit – staying under the rules of my Creator

About the Author 41

Contact Information 42

FOREWORD

How many times have you experienced that gnawing feeling on the inside that you were not getting everything you were supposed to have out of life? You felt that something was missing, but you were not able to figure it out and tap into a life that is full of possibilities. In *The Key to Transformed Thinking*, Ron Daugherty gives us insight into his process of becoming as he embarks on his journey to transformed thinking.

When I was asked to review this work by Daugherty, I was first excited. The excitement became a challenge; however, when I saw the title, it quickly reminded me of my own transformational process. The process of transformation and the renewing of the spirit of the mind will be one of, if not the most, difficult experiences of your life. The question to be asked of you, by you, and for you is: are you willing to endure the pain of transforming your thinking in order to enjoy the pleasures of having a transformed mind?

Daugherty's testimony of transformation starts in his cocoon of incarceration. It is in this cocoon that the caterpillar dies and the butterfly comes to life. It was inside the cocoon and incubation chamber of the Jefferson County Jail that he got connected to his life support system. It was in his place of isolation during this wilderness experience that he ceased to be who he had been socialized to be and transformed into who he was created to be. The renewing of the spirit of his mind was the foundation for his transformation.

Daugherty tells us, when we transform our thinking, our entire world undergoes a process of radical change. The process will be painful, lengthy, lonely, and occurs in a place of isolation. But how amazing to discover that the rewards are greater than the pain because the very thing that holds you captive during your process of transformed thinking becomes the very thing that equips and prepares you to fly!

The Key to Transformed Thinking will release the overcoming power of Christ in the hearts of all who read, receive, and apply these principles in their lives. I believe the power contained within the pages of this book will be a key component as you start your journey to discover *The Key to Transformed Thinking*.

I highly commend Daugherty for this most valuable contribution to the Kingdom of God, and I pray that you discover "The Key to Transformed Thinking" in your own life.

> Dr. Larry Carnes
> Larry Carnes Ministries Inc.
> Covenant Cutters Ministries International

INTRODUCTION

If there is anything the world needs today, it is transformed thinking. The impact of bad decision-making upon mankind has obscured our ability to think according to the truth. The reality is, apart from a vital connection with the Spirit of God, it is impossible for men, women, boys and girls to receive, understand, and apply truth.

According to the bible, ever since the Fall, humanity has been under the deceptive spell of the devil. Somehow, we find it easier to believe and absorb lies than the truth. Why? Because of man's bad decision-making, our nature is built upon the foundation of satan's lies. In particular, we fall prey to the original lie that brought spiritual death upon us all. In the Garden of Eden, the vile serpent convinced our first ancestors that they could become gods if only they ate the fruit of the very tree God had told them not to eat of. Since that time, mankind has suffered the consequences of rejecting the truth given by God in favor of a selfish desire to do things our own way, answering to no one.

The key to transformed thinking is restoring that original, vital, intimate relationship with God. This book seeks to guide its readers to have a God-conscious mental capacity to make godly decisions and to live in the unique holiness that God desires for us. This transformation is far more dramatic than the metamorphosis of a caterpillar into a glorious butterfly. It is the transformation of people whose minds were once hostile toward God into those who are captivated by the glory of His Word and His will for their lives. This is more than mere knowledge of the truth. It is a delight in it, a savoring of the experience of spiritual union through the work of God's Spirit.

Transformed thinking involves many things, including thinking God's thoughts, choosing God's will above our own, and presenting ourselves to Him for whatever purposes He has for our lives. It moves from lofty thoughts of Christ on His throne to the daily regimen of making good choices about caring for our bodies. This is practical holiness, which comes from following our Lord moment by moment throughout the day.

Transformed thinking comes about as we meditate upon God's Word until we are saturated with its truth. It is taking old thoughts that were corrupted by negative influences and replacing them with the purity of God's Word. Our lives are filled with impossible challenges and difficult decisions and, without the wisdom of God, we would inevitably fail. But with God, all things are possible to those who believe.

Within these pages, you will be introduced to the transformative power of God's Spirit. You will undergo the special experience of being baptized in the Spirit so that you are enabled to live above your natural capabilities. You will be impacted by the Author of the Word from within the depths of your being and empowered to live a life that is shaped by transformed thinking. The truth becomes more than a collection of ideas: it unfolds as a relationship with the One who is Truth.

Ron Daugherty

Chapter 1

TRANSFORMATION

*A transition in form, nature, or character – going from
one behavior to a better one through process and time*

Renewing our Minds

Through Christ Jesus, our Creator has offered us the priceless gift of receiving His heart and sharing His love with others. It's His love that is totally unconditional and providing. Through renewal, it is no longer self-seeking love we offer but we share the love of Christ. The flawed human nature can be transformed into His perfect divine nature. But this is a process and doesn't happen overnight.

Let me explain. We are essentially spirit-beings, who live in a body and function through our soul, which is made up of our mind, our will and our emotions. Before we accepted Christ's teachings, our decision-making was driven by our will/appetite/desires, mind/intelligence/thinking, and emotions/feelings/attitude. Our spirit lay dormant and unconnected to the Spirit of God. But the moment we received Christ as our Lord and Savior, our spirit became instantly alive and was united with the Father. Suddenly many things which were a mystery to me became so plain because my spirit connected to the One who created me. I heard someone say, when you want positive results and performance, do not take a car to an outside manufacture; take the car back to its maker. We should always go back to our Maker when life is not moving in the right direction.

I remember thinking as I lay inside the walls of hell that I was about to lose my mind. I asked the One who created my soul to assist me in keeping my mind. He gave me a word after weeks and weeks of tears and emotional pain. He said, "The penalty of bad choices, Ron, has totally desensitized you." I was separated from the very source that could give me everything my heart desired, but I didn't know what I was hungry for.

That word resounded in my mind and body like the turned up volume from the reverb and speakers of a sound system. The word echoed the cost of so many defeatist decisions that take your energy away. I didn't understand at first, that uncontrolled substance abuse of drugs, wild parties, women and illegal trafficking of money, had killed me, cut me off from the joy that was so close in me. I learned my spirit has some good but my soul has to be nourished so that my soul can obey my spirit. The One who created us is Spirit; He is the Word, and the words He says to us give us life. All the words that we hear do not always give our soul life.

When we don't have the Spirit of the One who gave us spirit, body and soul, our soul still lags behind, held captive to our old habits and patterns of thought, and unwilling to change. Our spirit longs to break out and explore the things of God but our soul, our "flesh," still wants to indulge in its former pursuits. Why has the bible told us to be transformed by the renewing of our minds? Because through it we learn to overcome every obstacle that desires to defeat us.

Let me share with you what I mean by transformed thinking. I started smoking cigarettes when I was a teenager. I declared I would smoke until the day I died. I'm not saying smoking will keep you out of His presence but, in my case, my smoking was for life. I started a 24-hour fast July 31, 1988. On August 1, 1988 24 hours later, I heard a voice say to me, "If you can go 24 hours without a cigarette you can go without it the rest of your life." Today is October 22, 2019. I have not had, tried to or desired a smoke since August 1, 1988. I am free from that addiction. YES!

How are we to be transformed? Mainly though the Word of God, spiritual exercising and meditation. Through the Word, the bible is like a parent. We spend time with the bible, and we recognize the voice. The more we exercise and meditate on the words of the bible, the stronger we get. Christ the anointed One speaks to us and enables us to know Him. We put our trust in Him and begin a close walk with Him. Through the Word, the Spirit of God teaches us the ways of God and gives us the faith to receive His strength to overcome difficult times and our destructive passions.

When our thinking is transformed, it is no longer bound by what our natural mind will see. We are taught to see into the things of the Spirit. We see with a panoramic view. Where we were once limited and captive to bad decision-making, we are now God conscious, allowing the Spirit of the One who made us to lead us. We are free and responsive because we focus on Christ, not on the pull of the old nature. Our thoughts are transformed, and we have the ability to overcome defeated mindsets and memories and live the highest form of life while here on earth.

We are now learning to think like Christ. What kind of mind is in Christ? He has a mind to love, laugh, and live the best life here on earth as if He were in heaven. Unfortunately, even as Christians, we tend to limit our thoughts only to things we can see in the natural.

However, God has told us to "seek the kingdom of God first" and He will supply all our daily needs. The kingdom of God is more than food and drink but peace, joy, and righteousness in His Spirit. The bible plainly tells us to think on things

> *When we are God-focused, things are beautiful because our thoughts are His thoughts.*

that are positive and life-affirming if we want to be powerful. When we are God-focused, things are beautiful because our thoughts are His thoughts.

The Metamorphosis of Thinking like Christ

Transformation is painful. Your first step could lead you to a place you would rather avoid. Making the decision to go through the process of working out your soul's salvation might be a huge struggle. It's called being alone, and I will share more about it in a later chapter.

A good example of transformation is a caterpillar turning into a butterfly, a process known as metamorphosis. Unlike reformation, metamorphosis is a total transformation of the substance and nature of a thing. The caterpillar wraps itself in a cocoon and is placed in an uncomfortable position that transitions life from crawling to flying. Remember, nothing but the chrysalis can break through the shell of the cocoon.

If the butterfly receives help from another source, it will lose its life.

In the same way, transforming to a new creation will require that you place yourself in an uncomfortable position. This could translate into a bad marriage, an unhealthy parental relationship, a difficult job, incarceration, drug or alcohol addiction, or a lack of finances. Whatever it is, it's very uncomfortable; but it is important to know you will not stay in that painful position forever. You may feel all alone, but, remember, the One who created you is always there for you. If anyone assists in the process, you could lose your mind. That means if someone who is not sent by God tries to control your transformation, the process will fail and you will remain in the same state – or you could die. People who get lost in the process could lose their minds and die to reality; they lose touch with the truth.

But God wants you to come out of the situation. He has created you to overcome – to float like a butterfly. A butterfly represents freedom. With transformed thinking, you are free, free from the control of wrong decision-making that entraps you.

Yes, it's our wrong choices that keep us from accomplishing our goals and dreams. However, when we let God transform us through His Spirit and His Word, we begin to break out of those negative choices. Fly butterfly! Fly! Now is your time to break free. I touch my faith with your faith and loose you from your chains. Receive the mind of Christ!

The Miracle of Transformation

The bible gives a wonderful example of transformation. Jesus' first miracle was transforming something natural that stepped into the supernatural. Believe it or not, He turned water into wine! At a wedding feast, they ran out of wine and came to Jesus. Jesus' mother told the servants to do whatever He instructed them. Jesus told the servants to bring the pots and fill them with water. They obeyed. Obedience is key to your miracle of transformed thinking. Thinking the way God thinks is a miracle.

When the water pots were filled, Jesus told the servants to take them to the master of the feast. As they went, the water turned into wine. The water represents bitterness and the wine represents sweetness.

Don't you want to go from an aching heart to a sweet way of thinking? I mean, your thoughts will become so pleasant that even your sleep will be sweet, even when everything around you looks like it's falling apart. Can you imagine being extremely stressed and overwhelmed by what life throws at you but, after your transition, brimming with life, joy, and peace? Is that possible? It is – if you relax and apply the principles I'm teaching you. Stop and think about the possibilities, not about the problem.

Therefore, meditate on the right things. Don't forget to get in a place where you are not distracted. The longer you focus on and apply God's way of doing things, the less likely you are to be distracted. Whatever God asks you to do – do it. Don't be conformed to the world's way of seeing and doing things, but be transformed by renewing your mind through the eyes of faith.

The Peace of Transformed Thinking

What does a new, transformed life look like? Transformed thinking is peace – nothing missing, nothing broken. It's having a focused faith-filled mind. It's a mind of love and compassion. A mind filled with hope and prosperity. A mind that upholds fairness and justice. A unified, not a divided mind. Most importantly, a new mind marked by obedience to the Lord. Now we love to do His will, not out of compulsion, but out of love for Him. His commandments are not burdensome; they are easy to keep.

God could only grant me peace through Jesus when I allowed Him to transform my mind. What about you? Will you remain trapped in the world's system, or will you be transformed by renewing your mind in Christ? The purpose of renewal is for you to live and think the way God thinks.

When we look into a mirror, whose face do we see? Our own, of course. We see the reflection of our old self with all its worldly thinking and selfish appetites. But when we look into the mirror of God's Word, we now see the face of God full of His glory. As we gaze at that image, we are transformed from glory to glory by the Spirit of the Lord. Our end goal is to be conformed to the image of Christ so that our mode of thinking and living echoes His.

One of the traps of the world's system is its preoccupation with the uncertainties of tomorrow. What will happen to me if I fail my exam? If I get sick? If I lose my job? If my spouse leaves me for another? All this breeds constant anxiety and worry about the future. But God tells us to be anxious for nothing. He wants us to trust in Him to provide for us in everything: our success, our well-being, our relationships. All we need do is to come to Him in prayer and make our request to Him with a grateful heart. When we come to God with this attitude of mind, the bible says that the peace of God, which goes beyond all human understanding, will flood our being. God's peace, not the world's peace, will guard our hearts and minds from being weighed down by the pressures of life.

A Testimony of Transformation

Before I found my freedom in Christ, I did not know what my soul was looking for. In fact, in February 1987, I was locked up in the Jefferson County Jail in Birmingham, Alabama, charged with "trafficking cocaine with intent to distribute." I was guilty as charged!

One year and one month later, I received my sentence: fifteen years in prison. The first time

I woke up in jail, I knew I needed help. All of my practical help had come to an end. During a night of sleeplessness, I came face to face with the problems plaguing me. I felt something twisting in my brain, like someone squeezing water out of a towel. I knew I was losing my mind. I began to cry out in my blanket pulled over my head, and I hoped no one would hear the noise I made. Still no tears.

I cried out to the Lord. I told God that if He let me keep my mind, I would serve Him for the rest of my life. Finally, I fell asleep. When I woke up the next morning, I was overwhelmingly grateful that I hadn't lost my mind. That night I went to the chapel for service, and there I gave my life to Christ. That's when the process that had been slowly building in me kicked into full gear.

I constantly went to the chapel throughout the entire month, going to the altar every time to dedicate myself to Christ. I called home and asked for a bible. The Lord began to work on me. For the next three years, two months, and twelve days, I concentrated only on the Word of God. As a result, God transformed my mind.

My brothers and sisters, I can testify to you that my whole life changed before my very eyes. I lived differently. My thinking was transformed and I thought, spoke, acted, and reasoned in a new way. That was incredible! I no longer depended on the world's system. That was over for me.

The month originally set for my release from prison was March 2003. Through the grace and mercy of God, along with the new way of thinking that came from Him, I was released on May 25, 1991!

After I regained my freedom, people told me I wouldn't like the Christian life I had chosen. It was too tough and demanding, and slowly I would slip into my old ways. But God has kept me. He has guarded my mind and my heart through prayer.

For over twenty years, I was involved in reaching the world as the pastor of an expanding faith-based church, and I was blessed to be part of an international platform. I even owned a lucrative business, which I gave up in 2001, though I still receive support from the company.

Alone, but Not Lonely

Through my life-saving experience, one thing I wasn't prepared for was to be alone. I learned how an eagle sharpens his gifts and renews his physical body. First, he goes to a high secluded place and waits until he has shed all the old feathers. The old feathers the eagle has are too heavy to exercise the abilities the eagle was created to perform. A man like an eagle must spend time alone, so he or she can prepare for life's purposes. God was getting me ready for the things He promised. I had to stay alone to get rid of the old heavy life that I created. The weight of guilt and shame would not allow me to use my gifts appropriately.

In life I have always desired to help and become a blessing to people. Why was spending time alone with the One who fashioned me after His image necessary? I used to get everything I wanted in life through sheer will power. I did not have to manipulate to get it. I could even inspire others and live without guilt – doing what I was doing, rather than feeling guilty. I would sell drugs and tell people how they could not find better drugs in the entire city. I also would tell people how they could make lots of money and how drug dealing would give them the good life. I never told them that drug dealing would also give them a bad conscience.

While spending time with my Savior, I learned to tell people about the good news of Gods laws and principles. He taught me how to go to the mountain top alone and get rid of the heaviness so I could fly higher than ever. I was taught how to sharpen my gifts in a way that my conscience would stay clear of guilt.

Spiritual Wisdom

My brother and my sister, I can assure you that, once your way of thinking is transformed, you will never be the same again. Here are some key principles from the bible that have changed me forever. I know they will work for you, too!

- Let the Word sink into your spirit and cleanse you from all your bad decision-making and weaknesses.
- Overcome whatever tries to control your thoughts by the power given to you by the Word.
- Think thoughts that are life-giving. The bible says that as a man thinks in his heart, so is he.
- Cultivate a mind that is full of the Spirit of God, and you will have life and peace.
- When your mind and emotions prosper, every part of your life will prosper to give glory to God.

- The Spirit of God within you is greater than the spirit that is in the world.
- Out of gratitude to God for His mercy, present your body to God as a living sacrifice. This means giving up bad decision-making and living a life that is set apart and acceptable to God. This is the least of what you can do for the One who saved you. And do not follow the ways of this world but be transformed by the renewing of your mind. This is the way you witness to the world that you are in that good, acceptable and perfect will of God.

Therefore, do not walk any longer like those who have walked away from Christ. Their thoughts are foolish and empty. Their understanding is darkened, and they are unable to see clearly. They have chosen to separate themselves from the One who created them. They have let hardness of heart and ignorance blind them to the truth.

Are you like the unbelievers wasting the mind God gave you? If you have allowed yourself to live by the dictates of this world's system, your understanding is indeed darkened from the life of God. This is a horrible condition to be in – especially when you know the truth. But there is hope. All you have to do is turn to God and practice what His Word tells you to do. In doing so, you will receive the freedom from bondage that He provides through His power.

By allowing Christ to transform your life, you do not lose anything. Instead, you gain everything by following the Lord. He can do much more than you could ever ask or imagine because of His power working in you.

Chapter 2

HOLINESS

Consistently making the right choices

> *Tell yourself you will no longer let the thing you abused control your life.*

In this chapter, we will assist you in understanding what it takes to make good decisions consistently.

The first thing we should do is to present our bodies as a living sacrifice, in a way that is holy and acceptable to God. When we refuse to do so, there can be no transformation. You decide how you want to treat your body, and whether you will care for it according to God's design. Before you can transform any part of your life, you have to make a choice and follow the process.

Holiness is Required

I have found that, if you want to think like God thinks, it means choosing to live a disciplined life. Living a self-restrained life means you are living a blessed and devoted life to the One who created you. This means breaking away from the things which can harm you, and dedicating your body and mind to the anointed One who desires to remold you. It means cutting yourself away from many of your bad habits. Some people eat too much; or they abuse their bodies. Others worry too much or drink too much alcohol. Some complain and grumble all the time. Whatever the abuse may be, whether physical or psychological, it has a detrimental effect on your entire being.

God desires us to be successful in all things and enjoy good health in our body, and in our mind and emotions. Health plays a vital role in our total transformation. Without being conscious of why I was doing it, during the process of transitioning from my old conduct to my new way of life, I naturally started to work on my physical health first. Lifting weights, playing basketball and running became a part of my regimen.

For many, the transformation process may initially bring pain because we are giving up many things we previously enjoyed. It could be over-indulging in food or alcohol, or spending your time partying or watching porn. Separating yourself from these things will naturally be difficult at first. But the Holy Spirit will get into your spirit and cause those past interests to fade away. He will fill you with new wholesome thoughts and desires that bring life.

When we waste away our time on useless things, we become separated from God. When a person ignores God's law, that person cannot see spiritual things and most of the time lives by his or her own feelings. People can become greedy, wild and display unwholesome behavior. Let me tell you how to fix any undesirable behavior. Get rid of the old conduct; determine that your lifestyle is unwholesome and detrimental to the laws of successful living. In all the laws to living, God calls us to disciplined living. Be divine because God is divine.

For God did not call us to immoral behavior but desires that we live clean and disciplined lives. When we reject purity, we reject the One who designed us. Make the decision to present your body to Him holy consistently and get your mind free from the bondages brought upon you by poor choices. Tell yourself you will no longer let the thing you abused control your life.

Finding Balance in Transformation

When we find the balance of living fresh and healthy lives, we have peace. Without structure and peace, we cannot have the correct image of God. Without self-discipline, we cannot experience lasting harmony.

Living a blessed life will cause God to take you back and use you in situations that once caused you pain. He wants you to share your life story with others. The woman, whom Jesus met at the well, had been married five times. Once she knew Jesus, her life changed, and she went back to witness to her village that she found new life in Christ. The demoniac who received deliverance by Jesus went back to his hometown to witness to those who once knew him as crazy. The prodigal son came to his senses after living in poverty in a dump and went back to his family. It does not matter what your uncomfortable situation is. God can transform you if you make the decision to offer your life as a self-sacrifice.

Notice I have mentioned the word "balance" a few times. Sometimes, we think we are living blessed lives as we literally separate ourselves from everything and everyone for fear of them pulling us back to our old ways. That's not God's intended purpose for your transformation. After you have experienced the good life, you ought to share your story with others. Unfortunately, because we can be overly fascinated by the new life we have, we may sometimes keep to the company those who think like us. We need to beware of this tendency lest we are no longer relevant to society.

When you no longer desire the person, place or thing that has caused you pain, disappointments, and sometimes disaster, and you've found a balance in your new attractive life in God, you should be willing to share your experience with family, friends, and others. In doing so, the transformation you are undergoing will go from strength to strength.

A Place of Worship

Did you know that your body is a place of worship for the Holy Spirit? God created human beings to care not just for their souls but also for their bodies. God's desire is to transform us from a nature that makes bad choices to a God-choosing nature. Man's fallen nature desires to allow the five senses and all their appetites to determine his lifestyle. But the nature God wants us to have is determined by Him.

God created us in His image so we can make decisions that will not harm us. Yes, we will make some wrong choices even when we have a Christ-like nature. But this will only happen in instances when we are not guided by Him. At times, we get bored with the way we live, and we want to taste something different – more exciting? When we become less sensitive to the voice of God, we make bad choices. Remember, that our body belongs to the One who created us and we have to decide to live according to His rules and thus experience true transformation.

Holiness is not what you wear outwardly; it's what you put on inwardly. Inwardly, we make a choice to live according to God's Word. We embrace righteous decision making; it becomes a part of our thoughts, talk, and actions. We think clean; we talk clean, and we behave clean.

Chapter 3

MEDITATION

*Thinking about the solution until the
answer is rooted in you*

What does the Word say about meditating? We should meditate until we get the answers to your questions? The bible tells us to dwell on things that are good, noble, pure, and of good report. If we do this, the peace of God will come upon us. Serenity is the key to winning every battle. When life brings challenges too big to overcome, instead of moping about our circumstances, we should turn our eyes to a good story. That good story will remind us about the many times our Creator rescued us from danger. This will keep our minds secure and relaxed.

I remember the day I was about to lose my mind; it was a sinking hopeless feeling. I pushed to read the bible chapter by chapter. Eventually, I could literally feel waves of relief sweeping over my mind and entire body. God's Word has the power to transform you into someone fresh and joyful.

Let meditation become a way of life for you. The Bible's way of meditating is not like the methods prescribed by yoga and eastern religions. There you are told to empty your mind and center on a single word. But the bible tells us to mediate by filling our mind with God's Word and thoughts of good report. It tells us to mediate on God's Word continually so that it is rooted deep within our consciousness. Imagining continually on good things keeps us in check when we are tempted to give in to emotions of anger or lust.

Studying the Word

In the bible King David constantly reflected on the Word of the Lord. He often stayed awake at night dwelling on the promises of God. That gave him strength. We, also, can study and meditate on the Word. As a result, the words becomes a part of us. After meditating, we talk and act upon what we have been thinking so that the words can lead and direct us. If you think about God's promises long enough, the fruit of each thought will come alive in your speech and actions. In the same way, when you entertain negative thoughts, you will experience bitter fruit.

There was a time in my life when I did not know what to look for. I had no vision. My pains and defeats pushed me to study and meditate on the Word and there I found something I wasn't aware existed. I received a peace that brought sweet sleep, love that healed my soul, forgiveness that was refreshing, sharing and caring I never knew were possible. Thank God! I finally got it!!!

The Importance of Meditation

Why is it so important to meditate while going through the transformational process? Meditation is an exercise which requires a person to wait on God. It's an art that demands focus, patience, silence, and stillness. Waiting on God renews your spiritual strength. Remember the tattered eagle waiting patiently for its new feathers to grow. Then it can lift its wings and soar to greater heights. Waiting or meditating can give you the strength to soar, too. While contemplating, you are downloading important information into your spirit and soul. Such information can and should replace old thoughts and learned actions with new, energizing revelations.

Meditation reminds me of Joshua, Moses' successor, whom God chose to lead His people into the Promised Land. Like Joshua, God is reminding us to keep the Word in our mouths and to meditate on it night and day. Then our way would be prosperous, and we would have good success.

I want you to think about the times you were contemplating what to do about your challenges? What happens depends on the challenge, right? Not quite. It depends on how you choose to respond to the challenge. What if you went around all day thinking bad of the person who embarrassed or offended you? There is a strong possibility that your emotions would overwhelm you – perhaps you might be thinking about ways to get even. If you conceive of the thought, that is, if you meditate on the thought long enough, more than likely, your focus will turn into action. You have two choices: to react and strike back or to forgive and release.

During the hardest period of my life, it was meditation that helped me break out of a state of hopelessness. I learned the power and method of thinking on what I desired until it became a part of me. When thoughts of good report occupy the deepest parts of your mind, you will eventually see your healthy thoughts turn into healthy actions. Meditate – Root – Fruit.

What a person meditates on gets embedded in the subconscious. After the thought takes root in the deepest parts of your being, you reproduce what you were thinking.

In the darkest chapter of my life I learned to think, speak and behave my way to a blessed life. The process was painful, but the reward was potent. I am 60 years old and my life could have been over. I had made one decision that could have cost me 45 plus years of my life. All that changed when I grabbed on to the principles that I am teaching in this book and I use them today in any circumstance that comes against me. I encourage you to find the answer to your challenge and meditate on the answer. You can dream, speak and act upon the solution and see your way out.

The Manifestation of Meditation

When I was a little boy, I remember an incident when a man went out and killed a police officer. When asked why he killed the officer, his response was that he listened to and obeyed the song that kept chanting, "Kill the police." This story is true.

In my life, for anything I have wanted, I meditated on the desired result. Some things came fast and others took time; but if I thought, focused, and waited for the outcome, it happened – good or bad. However, don't be fooled into thinking that, because you have learned the art of meditation, you will get everything you want. Dr. Fredrick K.C. Price in his book, "Faith, Foolishness, and Presumption" asks a very pertinent question: Where are you when it comes to meditating?

In the Books of Psalms, the writer tells us to follow this pattern to control your thought life:

1. Avoid the advice of ungodly people who are directed by their own pleasures.
2. Don't live a life of inappropriate thoughts and actions.
3. Be careful of how you deal with people.

Apply the principles of the bible to your life. Think and act on godly advice and treat people in a way that brings about agreement and harmony. Enjoy living by these laws, and you will produce. Now, you will be like a tree planted by the rivers of water that brings forth its fruit in its season, and everything you do will prosper.

Spending Time with God

Spending time in the Word means spending time with God. Can you imagine how much a person could grow if he or she spent time meditating on God's Word? As a man thinks, so is he. Meditation can build your self-worth, self-esteem, and any other part of your life when there is lack. God is a Spirit, and meditating on His Word daily, helps us to commune with Him and receive His Spirit. Man is essentially spirit; he possesses a soul and lives in a body. God is a Spirit. God is the Word. God is Love!

Jesus says it is the Spirit/Word that gives a person the good life; the fallen nature profits us nothing. He goes on to say the words that He speaks to us are Spirit and life. God has words that He wants us to meditate on day and night. When facing dangerous times, think about what God has said. Be strong and courageous, for He promises He will never leave you, nor will He forsake you. We must train, condition, and press in to keep our thoughts centered on the promises of Christ. What shall separate me from God? Nothing!

For years I remained ignorant of the truth: God's thoughts were not my thoughts, and His ways were not my ways. But His ways and thoughts can become our ways when we learn to activate them. No one ever told me when we receive Christ's teachings in our hearts that we should strive to have the same mind as He. We know now that, when we think about Him consistently, our thoughts can be formed and shaped to be like His. The Word of God in a person's mind will come out of his mouth and produce miracles.

Chapter 4

BAPTISM IN THE HOLY SPIRIT

Abiding by the rules of my Creator

In this part of the book, I want to share with you the power of the Holy Spirit. The Holy Spirit is the Person that inspired the writing of the Word of God and He will inspire you the reader. He is the Spirit that gives life. While our old fallen nature does nothing for us, the words Jesus speaks to us through the Holy Spirit are spirit and life. God is a Spirit, and we must get in the Spirit of God to experience the baptism of the Holy Spirit. This is what I will explain in this chapter.

The Importance of Baptism/Discipline

The definition of discipline is control gained by enforcing obedience or order. Accessing the discipline that's needed to accomplish the best in life can only come with a self-controlled mind. Have you ever heard of being under a spell? What that means is we are controlled by a system or a way of repeating a situation continually.

In the church water baptism demonstrates repentance, which is turning from the direction you were going and moving in the direction you were created to go. The baptism/discipline of the Holy Spirit is demonstrated through our consistent humility and willingness to make Christ-like decisions because we have submitted to His rulership. Don't forget it is the teachings of Christ that successful people follow. For example, look at some of your greatest motivational speakers or the Oprahs of the world. People are now understanding how important their spiritual life is. The baptism/discipline I will speak about has the ability to transform a human being's complete life. When people experience transformation by the potency of God's Word through the enabling of the Holy Spirit, they will never be the same again. Their outlook on life, the way they talk, how they hear and respond will all be much different.

We know that the activation of the Word is life changing. The drive and motivation that words create give us miraculous power. The Holy Spirit can restore us even when we make mistakes. By spirit, I mean that the word of our Creator and Maker will change our character into the person God intends us to be. If you are a timid person, the Holy Spirit will make you a bold and brave one. The same Holy Spirit will take an overly aggressive person and make them calm and assertive, rather than forceful. The Holy Spirit will encourage you to abide in the Word, so you can follow Christ's teachings. You will know the truth and the truth will make you free. The Word will free all those who apply the principles diligently to their lives.

The Word is Truth

The Word of God is truth. When we accept Jesus and receive the baptism/discipline of the Holy Spirit, we are blessed because we are living in the truth. I use the word "blessed" – a word most people do not understand. "Blessed" means dedicating your life to the One who put you together and gets you to a place of making good choices consistently.

Jesus said that His words are spirit and life and have the power to cleanse. Now you are clean through the words He has spoken. Therefore, the only way to cooperate with the Holy Spirit working within you is to saturate yourself in the Word of God. The Holy Spirit always agrees with the Word. The Word will help you in all your struggles and will transform your thinking.

When I was a teenager, all I thought about was how to manipulate things and people for my own satisfaction. As I grew older, I made poor decisions that hurt me and negatively affected many around me. I did want to change my lifestyle but, not knowing how, I was not equipped to do so. It all came to a head when I made the choice of traveling across the state line with two kilograms and four ounces of undiluted cocaine. The choice hurt so many who loved me because I was arrested.

One year later, I decided to make a radical choice. I asked Christ to come into my life, and He showed up. I was looking for freedom from the situation I was caught in, but He gave me a liberty that I had never dreamed of.

A year later I was sentenced to 15 years in a state penal institution and nine months after that I was sentenced to 45 year in the federal institution. My life and family were devastated. About one year into reading, studying and seeking God, an overwhelming sense of freedom took control of my life – "the discipline." I became thankful and aware of the person I was becoming compared to the person I had used to be. My true self had never wanted to intentionally hurt anyone, but I failed time and time again. When I had found discipline through the bible, Christ gave me the ability to stay consistent in living an orderly life. I was able to stop hurting the people around me. The hurt wasn't physical; it had to do with the choices we made. The bad choices that I had carelessly drifted into were having children before marriage, getting high on drugs, not building a career to help people, and not furthering my education.

A New Way of Thinking

When a person is baptized in the Holy Spirit, he or she begins to look at things differently than before. Think about a corrupt politician. He goes through a crisis that pressures him into deciding he can't live that way any longer. Later, we are surprised to hear a testimony about this ruthless person changing from being an offender to a God-loving, people-serving, bible-believing new creation. Not only his thinking but also his actions are changed. If you practice living by the standards of the bible, God will take your weaknesses and replace them with His strength. He will replace your discouragement with encouragement. Staying under the power of Christ's rules will take you from timidity to boldness with balance. The discipline enriches you and gives you the ability to reproduce. Many people will be touched and changed because they see Christ in you. When the church talks about being baptized/disciplined in the Holy Spirit, we are saying that the Holy Spirit is in control. Another way of saying it is that the believer is immersed or put under the power of the Spirit.

The Holy Spirit helps the Word you apply become real, not just a set of rules. When the Word is spoken to us, we recognize it is God's voice, and we decide to follow Him. As we live out Christ's teachings from day to day, moment to moment, we gain the ability to live as the bible instructs us. God's voice can be heard in the spirit of our minds, through His Word, through people, or through situations. Christ desires for us to listen to his voice and obey Him through words, trials and circumstances. He says that His sheep know His voice and will follow Him. God's sheep will flee from the voice of "strangers."

If you are or were what some people call an "outcast," you will understand what I'm about to explain. There are street hustlers who control people, places, and things without sometimes understanding the authority they possess. Drug dealers use a substance that lures some people to the extent they can only see the tools and substance that take them to euphoric highs. They are baptized in a drug that has total control over their minds. The drug dealer can get some of the addicts to do anything. They become fanatic followers of his orders.

All I'm saying is we have been created to serve, love and live in a way that leads to great blessing. The way for us to get to the blessed life is follow the teachings of the One who created us. He asks us to do a few things that will transform our lives. He says treat your body with great respect. He also says your mind is a tool: if you think it, you can have it. If you can say it, you can see it. You will then be able to say, "Life is good. I got It!"

The God we serve has a substance called faith. When we take our faith and use it, God works for us. We attain a euphoric feeling and there is a desire to keep on using our faith. A believer who is baptized/disciplined in the Spirit respects and obeys the God of faith like no other person. Therefore, we must stay under the instruction of the One who made us. Now we can live by the standards of our Creator.

The purpose of the Baptism/discipline of the Holy Spirit (BOTH) is to keep us submitted to the teachings of Christ and doing things His way. I have been under the teaching of Christ for thirty years. The first twenty-seven years of my life were filled with pain. I fell from a car and fractured my skull, my mom and dad divorced, and I went to prison. However, since I've fallen in love with the Word of God, I have put my past in the past. I can honestly say today He has given me the good life.

Remember, God wants you to have a life of peace and prosperity. Decide to transform your life today by living a good decision-making life based on the Word of God, meditating on the

Word, and living in the Spirit of God. You might ask the question, "How can I accomplish what you have said to me?" This is how you do it:

- Present your body as a living example, disciplined, structured and acceptable to God. Do not get caught up in systems that trap and penalize you. Transform your thought life through the Word of God, not the world's corrupted system.

- Don't be anxious about anything, but in every situation pray and give thanks to God in advance for what He is about to do. When you do so, God's peace will guard your spirit and mind in Christ.

- Meditate on what God's Word says day and night, and you are guaranteed of prosperity and success.

- All your old bad habits will not bring profit; but the Word of God will give you life. The words that the Lord speaks to you are Spirit and life changing. Hide them in your heart.

Transform your thinking...transform your life!

ABOUT THE AUTHOR

Ron Daugherty represents a testimony to the restorative and transforming nature of God. Through submission to the power of the Holy Spirit, his obedience to follow God's plan for his life, and his willingness to go through the process, God is able to use him mightily. Daugherty is involved in international works and has become a shining light revealing the Lord's divine, redemptive power. Through Christ, he has helped many through restoration and the transformational process.

He holds a Bachelor of Arts degree in Leadership Studies from Beulah Heights University and an MBA in Communications and Marketing from South University. He also received his Life Coach training from Dream Releasers Coaching.

CONTACT INFORMATION

Ronald Daugherty
678.612.6080
broron59@gmail.com